CITY RIDERS

CITY
RIDERS

A Story of Riding and Friendship

Written and Photographed by

ROBERTA FINEBERG

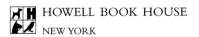 HOWELL BOOK HOUSE
NEW YORK

Howell Book House
A Simon & Schuster Macmillan Company
1633 Broadway
New York, NY 10019

MACMILLAN is a registered trademark of Macmillan, Inc.

Library of Congress Cataloging-in-Publication Data

Fineberg, Roberta.
    City Riders : a story of riding and friendship / written and photographed by Roberta Fineberg.
       p.   cm.
    ISBN 0-87605-728-8
    1. Show riding—New York (State)—New York.   2. Pendleton, Audrey.   3. Freundlich, Jenny.
4. Heymann, Chloe.   5. Claremont Riding Academy (New York, N.Y.)   I. Title.
SF295.5.F56   1997
798.2'4—dc21   97-5924
                                                                                                              CIP

Manufactured in the United States of America

10 9 8 7 6 5 4 3 2 1

Book design by George J. McKeon

To my son, Paris

CONTENTS

Foreword ix

1. AUDREY 3

2. JENNY 35

3. CHLOE 67

Acknowledgments 99

FOREWORD

There are certain girls for whom the obsession with riding is very strong. They can't get away from their desire to be around horses. Everything else in their lives becomes an inconvenience. School takes away from their time with horses; their horses begin to have more value for them than people. In other words, a dedicated young rider may start choosing her horse over people. There may be a horse who has peculiar habits . . . and then there will be that one little girl who responds to that horse—she will accept the horse. The horse may begin to change his behavior toward the girl—it's not a scientific relationship. The rider loves that animal, and the horse, in turn, returns her affection.

Horseback riding requires a lot of courage. A rider has to be capable of silent communication. Shakespeare once wrote, *no secret is so close as that between a horse and a rider.* You have to know how to read a horse—a look in his eyes, a flick of his ears or tail, and so on. Horses are capable of great levels of communication. A young rider has to know how to *reach* her horse.

"Pick one thing and stick with it" is a message I like to communicate to girls. Horses are my life. In my off time, I jump, show, and spend time with horses.

I think it's really important for girls to remain focused because there are so many distractions. Girls still remain unchallenged in many institutions, say, in schools.

Horses encourage girls to overcome difficulties and to grow. If it hadn't been for horses, I would have destroyed myself.

To succeed in riding—whether in showing or in racing—a girl also has to be good at mind and body control. She has to be athletic, in addition to knowing how to read silent signals. A rider has to be very aware.

A horse can be very restrained in a show situation. When you turn a horse loose that has been showing all day he will burst forth, leap in the air, shake, roll on the ground. Horses do become taxed while showing because it's a very controlled environment. A racehorse does experience, on some level, a natural feeling he would have in the wild—that is *to run*. There is a flight and fight mechanism at work in a horse in the wild. What makes horses bold and brave on the racetrack is their natural instinct to jump around, fight, and kick. You would be surprised if you visited a horse's stall at a racetrack; the groom is as attentive to him as he would be with a show horse. I have seen a lot of very pampered horses at the racetrack. There are those who are asleep every afternoon in three feet of straw! They come out of their stalls, yawning and wondering, "Who can I bite today?"

Racetracks get a bad rap because there is the old stereotype, "Is the racetrack a place for a girl?" Girls are my greatest fans. Although I have always considered myself a genderless athlete, I am recently comfortable saying *I'm a female jockey,* and I enjoy inspiring girls to take riding seriously.

Julie Krone

AUDREY

Chloe Heymann (left), 16, Jenny Freundlich (right), 15, and myself Audrey Pendleton (center), 14, have been friends since the fifth grade. Our friendship is based on a shared love of horses and horseback riding. We spend much of our free time in Manhattan at Claremont Riding Academy where we have formed a community. Chloe, Jenny, and I are best friends. We're like a family of three sisters.

Claremont is our clubhouse. We call it the barn. It's a relatively small riding academy, but it's the only stable in Manhattan—and I can't wait to get there after school. Even when a riding lesson is difficult, I'd rather be at the barn than anywhere else. Claremont, located on 89th Street at the corner of Amsterdam Avenue, is over 100 years old and became a public stable in the early 1930s. The barn is a brief trot to Central Park's extensive network of bridle paths. When school becomes demanding because of too many hours of homework or when I get, say, into arguments, I start thinking of Claremont.

Our instructors affectionately call us "barn rats." There are a few dozen barn rats at Claremont—those of us who ride often, work at the barn, or just hang out there. Then, there is David, our 11-year-old mascot and the only boy in the group. The barn rats have accepted him into the all-girl group because he's always willing to offer a helping hand.

Allison Estes (*left*) and Ellen Cargan (*right*), both in their thirties, have been riding their whole lives. They are trainers at Claremont and can

be both tough and tender with their students. They're our friends, confidantes, and mentors. They take us seriously and believe in us. We may not have the space at a city stable to jump high fences, but thanks to Allison and Ellen we've mastered the basics.

TRAINERS

When we're not riding, we spend hours working in the barn—grooming horses (currying, brushing, and bathing them), mucking out stalls (cleaning the stalls), and sending horses up and down the ramps from the stalls to the ring, where riders take lessons at all levels (from basic equitation to jumping and dressage).

Brushes, curry combs, and hoof picks are some of the items in a grooming box. Riders at Claremont have their own grooming boxes, and will almost exclusively groom their favorite horses.

Unlike the serenity offered by a stable in the country, the city barn is surrounded by skyscrapers, traffic, and concrete—an unusual environment for horses. Defying exhaust-spewing automobiles and buses, we, the adventurous trio, make our way into Central Park for an hour hack on the six miles of winding bridle paths.

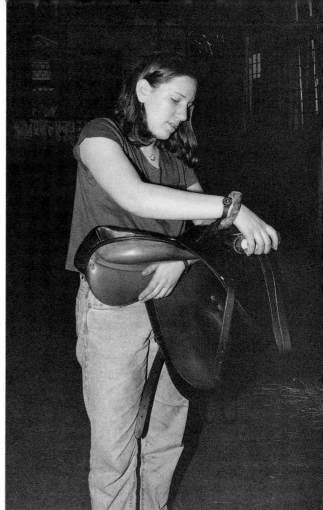

The cost of the sport? It's an activity you love so much, you're willing to make sacrifices. To earn money for riding we work after school and on weekends at Claremont. Four hours of work in the stable can be redeemed for one hour of riding time.

Chloe, Jenny, and I spend our summers earning money for lessons by helping to instruct campers at Overpeck, a stable in Leonia, New Jersey, 20 minutes from New York City. Being trainers as well as students gives us added insight.

There's always a moment of panic for a student when a horse acts up. The teacher has to remain calm and firm in order to instruct the student to lean back and shift her weight to the horse's hindquarters. It's sometimes easier to teach than to be a student.

I enjoy teaching at Overpeck. It excites me to pass on information and my love for horses to the kids. I've also learned how to deal with people who have less riding experience than me.

Mucking out stalls
(removing horse
manure and wet bed-
ding, then replacing it
with clean bedding—
either straw or cedar
shavings) is the least
desired task performed at summer camp, or anyplace, but it's essential
for the health of the horse.

Chloe, Jenny, and I taught the campers that cleaning out a horse's
stall is a necessary daily chore.

At camp we learn how to pick out a horse's feet (scraping loose the caked dirt from between the hoof and horseshoe with a hoof pick). It's not at all uncomfortable for the horse. In fact, he reacts favorably once the job has been completed by either a rider or a groom (someone employed to ready horses for riding) at a stable. A horse may need to have the dirt removed as often as three times a day because a nail, dirt, or a rock wedged in a hoof can create an infection.

Sasha Novagrad is a born rider. Yet, she takes lessons like other campers in Leonia. When the counselors aren't looking, Sasha loves to mount her pony, Mahoney, bareback. But, no one is supposed to know about her secret passion for riding Mahoney without a saddle. Sasha is as frisky as her pony and likes to take a few risks now and then.

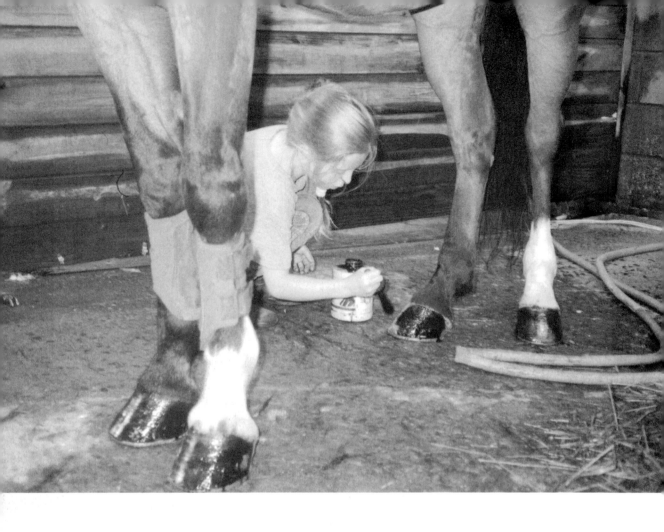

Sasha uses dressing to paint the hooves of her
pony. Think of it as a pedicure—it keeps
Mahoney's hooves shiny and moist.

Sasha cools off Mahoney.
He's cross-tied to the stall
while she hoses him down.
Sasha has to be careful not
to spray his face with water
because generally horses
don't like to get their faces
or ears wet.

Converse is heavy on his forehand (his front legs). That's where he puts most of his weight. When jumping, I first try to get myself balanced—it's completely unreasonable to ask the horse to balance himself unless I'm in balance. It's my responsibility to control him. A lot of work has to be put into a horse to make him a good jumper.

Before a show, there is a great deal of small talk in the locker room, ranging from, "Where is my boot?" and "Oh, no! I've got a rip in my britches," to, "I can't get my blouse buttoned!"

Although dressage outfits are pretty conservative, we sometimes goof off while wearing them.

TURNOUT

Before a show, you use a net and bobby pins to neatly arrange your hair. Then you stuff your hair in your helmet.

Jenny, Chloe, our friend Marianne, and I were in Thomas School for a two-day show. We spent a night at a nearby hotel. On the first day of the competition, we rode in the hunter/jumper show. That evening at the hotel we talked, watched TV, and did about ten seconds of homework.

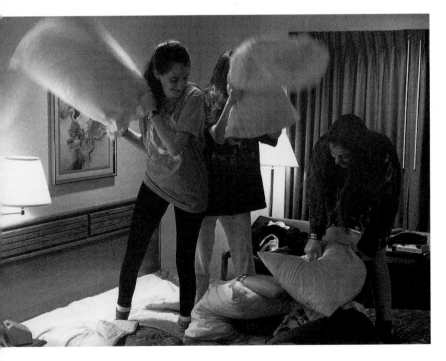

FUN

We had to share beds at the hotel the night before the Junior Olympics because there were four of us and only two beds—and if you do the math. . . . I am the youngest of the group, but nobody makes me feel like I'm too young. The following day Jenny on Acadia, Chloe riding Quincy, and I, with my horse Tuskers, were on the same team in the Junior Olympics. We were lucky; we won bronze medals.

At an Overpeck horse show I rode Pay Dirt in the pleasure division.
Here, a judge looks at how a horse performs on a longer rein. Tuskers
was off that day. But Pay Dirt and I wound up being champions.

I also showed in an equitation class.

My horse was Blaze.

BLAZE

At Claremont, we play the egg-and-spoon race. It's a relay race. I am riding Bo-Peep and trying to make sure the egg stays on the spoon while I go as fast as possible from one end of the ring to the other.

Tuskers is my favorite horse. He's very sweet and strong. He's fun to ride, and he likes to jump. He's great. I am the only one who rides him at Claremont besides his owner, Pam, the barn manager.

I ride Tuskers nearly every day. I give him one day off when I hand-walk him around the ring. In summer, I take Tuskers to Central Park six or seven days a week, where I ride him for an hour or more. Tuskers adores the Park.

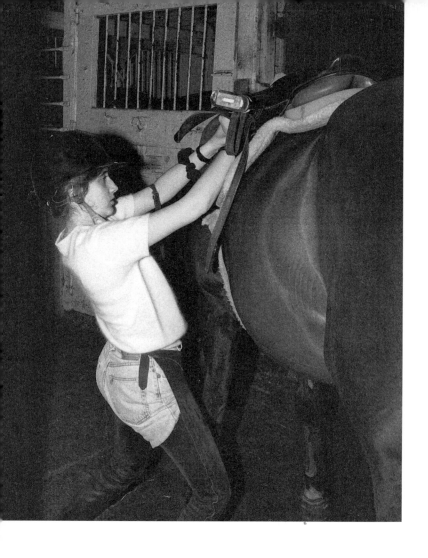

I am tightening Tusker's girth and getting him tacked up in preparation for a ride. A lot of horses will kick in protest. Tuskers doesn't seem to mind having a big strap tightened around his stomach.

Equitation isn't exactly a solo sport. Your teammate is your horse.

One of Audrey's goals is to enter the Medal-Maclay Finals at the National Horse Show, which is held at Madison Square Garden in New York City.

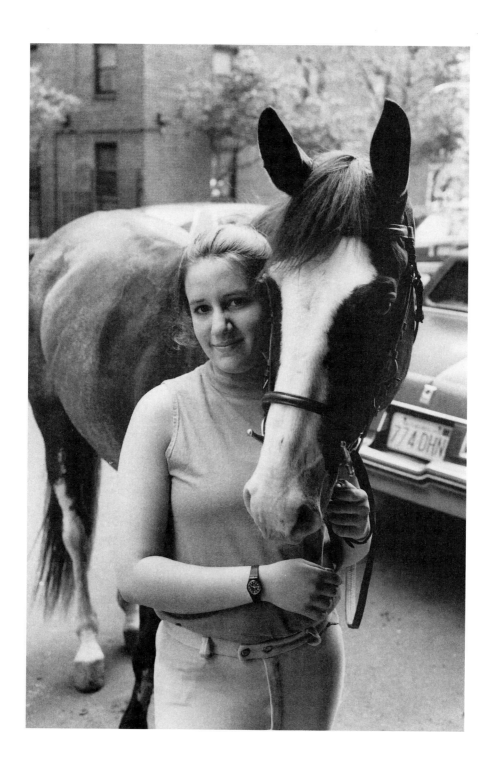

2

J ENNY

Most kids at the barn don't have their own horses, so they become adaptable and learn to ride many horses. City riders learn to be flexible. During the school year, it's easier to think about horses than to be with them. I'm only in the 10th grade, but homework takes up much of my time. I get over to the barn on weekends for my lessons and at least once during the week. It would be too costly for me to leave the city during the week or even on weekends to ride in the country.

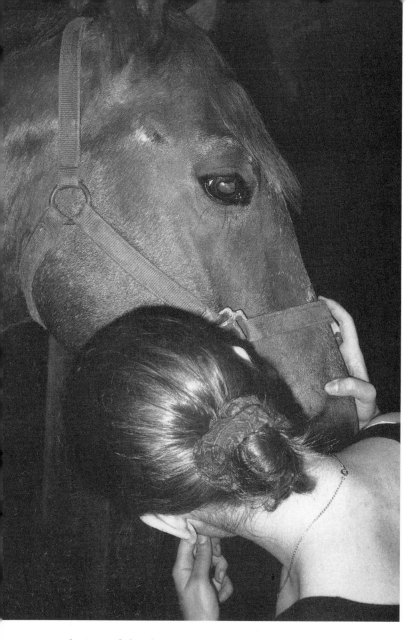

One of my favorite horses is a 20-year-old gelding named Legacy. My friends claimed that the minute I slid into the saddle, it just clicked. Legacy and I were a perfect match. I loved Legacy, he trusted me, and I trusted him. I used to enter his stall and talk to him. I would tell him all my problems. Because of his advanced age, Legacy can no longer work at Claremont. I have always felt that Legacy is very special, and so I wanted to help him. I became involved in the Willow Fund, an organization devoted to saving horses that are too old to be ridden.

The Willow Fund recognizes the need to place school horses in retirement homes when they can no longer be ridden. When we take horses out of the wild, we assume responsibility for them, including providing for their needs after their working years are over. Partly because of my intervention, Legacy was retired to Upstate New York, where he now enjoys grazing in fields.

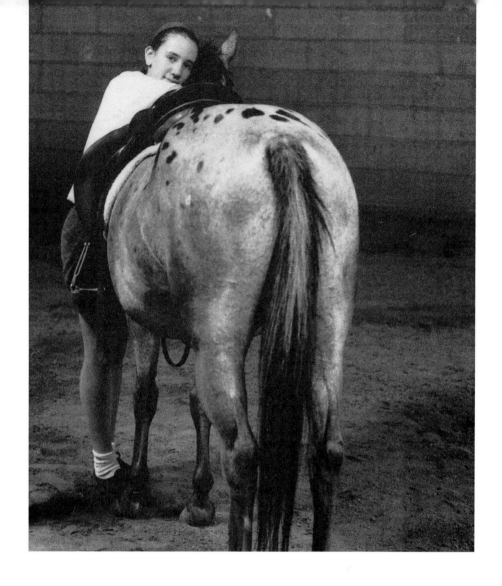

Horseback riding has helped me to become independent. I've learned that if you're not physically and emotionally comfortable on the horse's back, you're not going to feel secure. I've applied to life what I've learned in the riding ring.

Acadia is one of my favorite horses and one of my best friends, too. I love lots of things about him. He has a quiet nature—he doesn't pull funny stuff. Sometimes when Acadia has excess

energy, he will buck and play. A rider can fall in love with her horse.

Unlike a dog, a horse will not jump on you to greet you. But if you arrive every day at the same time to feed him in his stall, he will come to expect you. When I arrive at Acadia's stall he first bows his head down for me to groom his face. I don't know if Acadia misses me when I leave the barn, but he sure looks happy to see me return the next day. Horses thrive on routine.

A horse can't speak, but he does communicate by using body language. Pinned ears, wringing tail, and a hollow or humped back are all signs of tension.

You can tell what a horse is feeling.

ACADIA

My half-hour lessons with Allison provide an opportunity for self-improvement. We try to improve our form, not only for shows but also for ourselves.

Allison's jump class was great.

GREAT!

Chloe, Audrey, and I are in different grades, but the barn has a way of bridging gaps. At Claremont you can have relationships with kids as young as three years old or with adults two or three times your age.

We are like a portable party; we have
fun everywhere. We leave the barn at
7 P.M., and by 7:30
P.M. we are already
on the telephone
with each other.

The three of us have spent so much time together that we have ended up playing major roles in one another's lives. The three-way friendship has a lot of potential because three brains are better than one.

RELAXING

We're cleaning tack with saddle soap and a bucket of water. Doing anything with Audrey and Chloe is a lot of fun, and having horses around only strengthens our friendship. They share my love for horses, which means they understand a big part of me that other people may not.

A good piece of tack, for example a saddle or bridle, is a real investment. If you take care of it, it gets better over the years.

TACK

Halters are used when grooming a horse—or when the horse is hanging out in his stall. It is essential to have a horse's halter at hand in case of an emergency in the barn. Getting a horse out of a burning barn, for example, is no easy feat. Horses tend to want to return to their stalls where they feel safe, even if a barn is on fire. In a dangerous situation, a rider may have to blindfold a horse to get him to exit quickly from the stable.

The trails in Central Park are beautiful. It's
great to ride outside, especially in good
weather. A gorgeous day is certainly a gift to
riders who want to go trail riding in the Park.

Sniffing noses is how horses say hello to
each other.

CENTRAL PARK

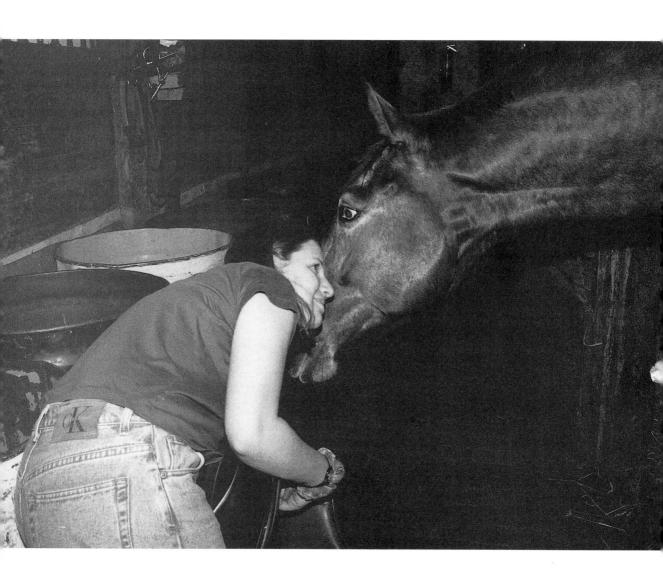

Horses are athletes, and they can share their speed and power with you for a little while. Their physical presence is both impressive and endearing. You have to learn how to work with your horse because you become two minds and two bodies cooperating as one. A rider makes the executive decisions while the horse maintains his position as the athlete. Horses don't understand shows, ribbons, or trophies—but they do enjoy the partnership with their riders.

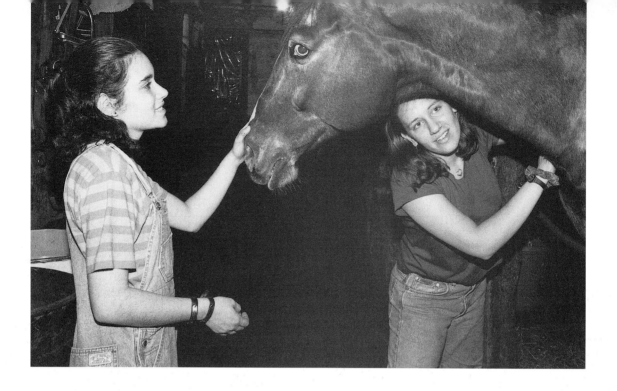

Horses enjoy being social as much as we do.

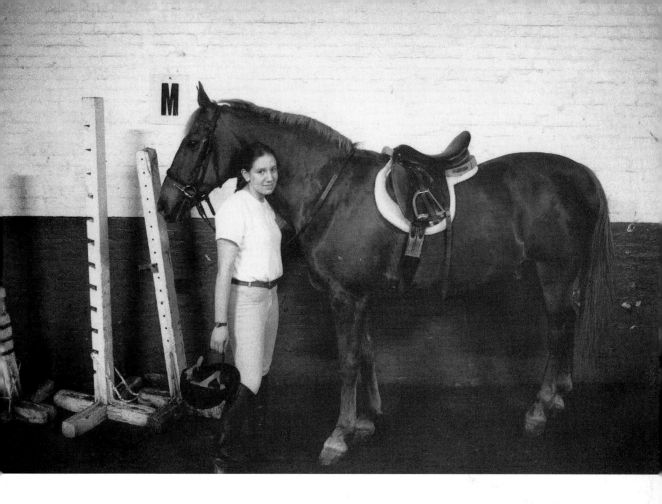

Paddington has been at the barn for years. He's one of the first horses people learn to ride, and thus has a special place in the hearts of many riders. He's a character, and it's not easy to learn how to ride him. PADDINGTON

I began riding Thursday a short time ago. The first time I rode him was in the Park for the Summer Solstice Ride. I took a shine to him. Generally I fall for the same type of horse—quiet Quarter Horses you can count on. Thursday likes to be in the lead of a large group, unlike Acadia who is perfectly happy to hang back.

Blaze is one of my favorite horses too. He is very sweet and loves to play with people. He was bought recently and is no longer a school horse at Claremont.

LOVE

Here's girl and horse—clearly friends. The more time I spend around horses, the crazier I am about them.

PARTNERS

The barn manager organizes a group from Claremont that shows at other barns. That group is called the Show Team. We rent a big trailer to bring the horses from Claremont to the show. Our trainers come along, too.

Making a horse show work is a big, big job. Shows can go all day and continue well into the night. A lot of people are behind making shows work, and the gateperson is one of them. The gateperson is responsible for opening and closing the gate—to let people in and out of the ring as quickly and smoothly as possible. They call riders in turn for their course and announce the order for riders on deck. If a horse is scheduled to show in two rings at the same time, the gateperson straightens out the problem. The ringmaster has the job of calling out to the riders in the class what it is the judge wants them to do. If the judge wants a rising trot, she whispers or signals to the ringmaster, and it's the ringmaster who makes the announcement.

There is a level of anxiety when competing in shows. The competition may be stiff. A competitor may be nervous about her ride and fear how she will place in a class. A rider and her horse perform for a judge. Sometimes nervousness can have a positive effect on your performance. It can drive you to do your best. If a rider is prepared, however, she can remain confident. In turn, confidence helps your ride.

RIBBONS

I'm taking a long bungee cord of ribbons off the trailer. I came along to help the Show Team. There's an enormous amount of work involved in bringing 10 horses and 20 people to a show.

Claremont barn manager Pam and trainer Allison display the ribbon that Claremont rider Sydney won. Sydney held the place after Champion. She was awarded the Reserve Champion Ribbon. Only two ribbons were awarded in the very tough hunter class in which Sydney rode Cartier to his victory.

We're packing up to go home. Coming along for the day was loads of fun.

Here, we've reached the end of another long day at the barn. We're tired, in need of a shower and dinner.

Jenny would spend every day at the barn if she could. She knows horses will remain in her life forever.

3

C H L O E

Acadia is one of Jenny's favorite horses. I love three horses—Quincy, Sweet Baby Jayne, and Piper, whose name I wear on a my leather horse bracelet. It took eight months before I realized how attached I was to Piper, an 11-year-old Appaloosa. It wasn't love at first sight, but I slowly became drawn to his personality. Piper was easygoing and dependable—an excellent school horse. Then I had the bracelet made. My mom came with me to Miller's, the equestrian shop in downtown Manhattan, and we picked up my first horse bracelet, with Piper's name inscribed in brass. Audrey used to feel bad that she didn't own a horse, but now she feels—as we all do—that she has 60 horses (the total number of horses at Claremont). Audrey's favorite horses are Tuskers, Seaview, and Quasar. Audrey had to narrow down her final choices to Tuskers and Seaview for her two horse bracelets.

Piper, my favorite horse at
Claremont, is now in
Connecticut because he became
too old to be a school horse at
the barn. My favorite place to PIPER
ride him was Central Park
because Piper was sluggish in
the ring. He preferred being
on a nice long rein in the Park,
where he felt comfortable.

Jenny and I like to go on hacks in the Park. It's more fun to ride there in small groups. Horses sometimes get spooky in city streets. It takes time for them to become used to cars and trucks. A rider has to keep her eyes focused on everything—other people, joggers, dogs, and kids—and she has to know how to control her horse should he spook. I take different horses to the Park, where I can canter and trot freely, depending on the footing. Central Park is the best place to ride in the  city. The best places to ride in the Park are on the north and south loops and around the Reservoir.

HACKS

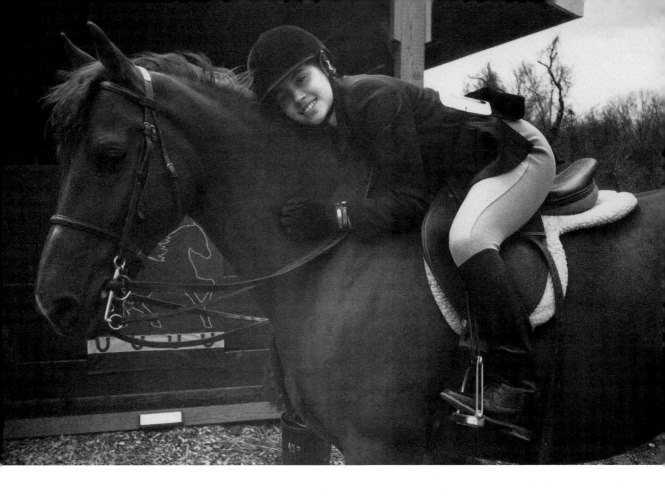

Riding involves my mind, body, and emotions—I have to know where I'm going and gauge my pace and rhythm. Participating in a sport can be as intellectually stimulating as a history lesson.

Allison's open jumper class, in which all levels may participate, takes place every Saturday morning. In Allison's class I am riding a very sweet pony named Vasco. He likes to jump, even though the turns at Claremont are tight and the jumps are not very big. Nevertheless, horses like to jump, even in small rings.

During a lesson Allison insists that her students work hard at their form, a task made more difficult by the jungle of poles and the dimly

lit, sometimes crowded ring. I've earned a number of blue ribbons at shows. Allison has shown me that I can succeed. I had to learn self–confidence, which Allison taught me by  instilling the notion that I should never give up on myself. Allison is my instructor, but she is also my friend.

ALLISON

Jenny and I have our lessons with Allison back-to-back on Saturday afternoons. I like to watch Jenny during her lesson. In between lessons, I share jokes with Allison.

I don't own a saddle. I borrow one from my friend Marianne. Most riders at Claremont borrow saddles. Having your own saddle is certainly nicer because you don't have to spend so much time adjusting the stirrups when you ride. Riding is expensive, and buying your own equipment costs a lot of money.

It's best to wear a boot or a shoe with a heel when you ride. If you wear a hard leather boot, there is less chance of getting hurt. A field boot is a tight-fitting high leather boot worn at horse shows by older kids and adults. A boot pull is necessary when putting boots on, while a boot jack is needed when taking them off.

Horses wear many kinds of shoes. If a horse's shoe comes off, you may not be able to ride or work him. A horse's shoes should be changed every six weeks. It's good luck to display a horseshoe with the open end facing up.

If you take horseback riding seriously, you've got to expect that eventually you will get bucked off or fall from a horse. And when you're thrown, you'd better be wearing a riding helmet. If you're not hurt, you climb back on. You have to accept the fact the horse is larger and more powerful than you. If you're afraid, don't let the horse know.

HELMETS

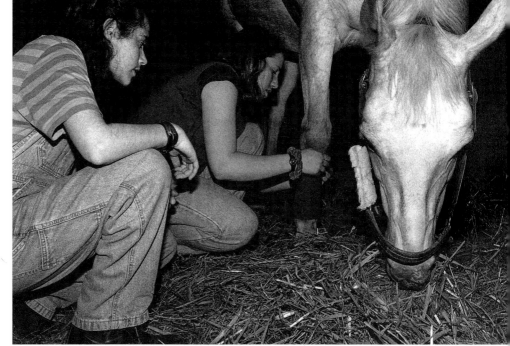

Polo wraps are supportive bandages a horse wears while he is being ridden. Wraps are not decorative; they protect the tendons in the back of a horse's legs. The front legs support a large percentage of a horse's weight. You have to tighten the wrap against the bone as opposed to the tendon.

An incorrectly applied bandage offers no support and can even damage a horse's leg. A bad wrap can hurt a horse.

Most barns have cats to keep away the mice. Barn cats may also drag in a bird or two from the out-doors. Among the cats at Claremont there is an orange tabby whose name is Pumpkin, a gray cat called Mouse, and an all-time favorite white cat that answers to the name Kitty Kelly.

The purpose of a horse show is to exhibit what you and your horse have learned. No one may be in the ring with you, even if somebody is encouraging you from the sidelines—like my mom, who comes to all my shows. In the end, you have to make your own decisions. As for the judges, they only see the finished product. A judge may not realize that you have put in years of work. The horse and I work for a common goal, and together we try to reach it safely and effectively.

JUMP COURSE

The way you learn a jump course at a show is by memorizing it from a piece of paper posted at the ring. There may be times during a competition when you forget the course, go off course, or become flustered. It's like forgetting your lines in a play.

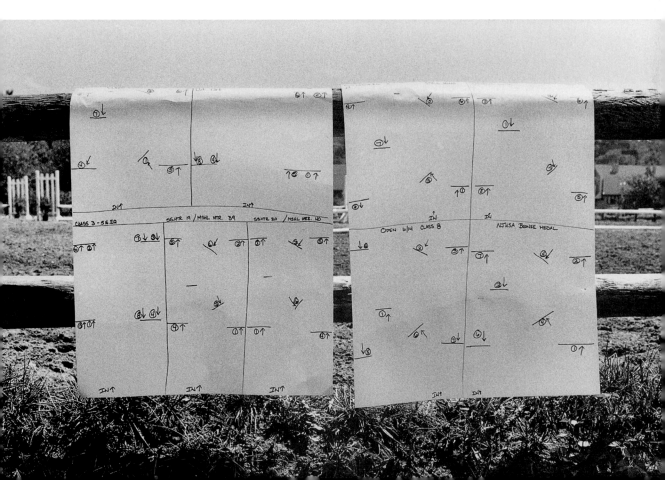

Jumper riders often carry jumping bats; longer whips are used in dressage. Crops and spurs are called artificial aids. Natural ones—such as your leg, seat, and weight—are also used to communicate with your horse. A crop is like an extension of your leg. It reinforces the message you want to give your horse if he doesn't respond to the squeeze of your legs against his sides. Crops are not used to punish the horse.

In equitation, riders are judged on their form.

The horse's mane has to be pulled or braided before shows. Sometimes you use a pulling comb to thin or even the mane. For braiding, you need to use yarn and a pull-through. Braiding takes a long time if you want to do a good job.

When you show, you think entirely about your performance. You have so much to consider, you can't daydream. You have to memorize the course, contemplate each approach, and consider how you're going to navigate the turns. When timed on a jump course, you have to decide the quickest and safest way around the course. To succeed, you have to stay focused.

There is a lot of standing around and socializing at shows. It never gets boring. There's always something to do—memorizing your course, watching other riders, taking care of your horse. . . .

FREE TIME

We showed our favorite horses from Claremont at Overpeck. My horse was Quincy, Audrey had Tuskers, Jenny took Acadia, and our friend Marianne rode Tio. Quincy sometimes spooks at fences, but at this show he jumped all the fences, and we won two events.

After shows at Claremont, the barn rats like to leap over the horse jumps. Max does a front hand-spring over one of the bales of hay.

We showed our favorite horses from Claremont at Overpeck. My horse was Quincy, Audrey had Tuskers, Jenny took Acadia, and our friend Marianne rode Tio. Quincy sometimes spooks at fences, but at this show he jumped all the fences, and we won two events.

I sit back, but try not to lean too far backward. I don't let myself get ahead of my horse either, because if he stopped suddenly, I would fall off.

When Quincy is good, he is very, very good. He went well that day in the pleasure class at Overpeck. Riders often go on pure adrenaline. At this show I didn't win a ribbon, but I felt I rode well. I was really in sync with Quincy.

Show's Over

Quincy seemed pretty tired because he had been ridden a lot at the show. I felt exhausted, too.

After shows at Claremont, the barn rats like to leap over the horse jumps. Max does a front hand-spring over one of the bales of hay.

Another Claremont event is the annual Halloween Ride. Riders and their horses dress in costumes and form a parade that criss-crosses Central Park, where the group walks, trots, and canters. One year Jenny was a fairy and her gray mount came as a unicorn, Audrey dressed as Minnie Mouse (her horse was Mickey Mouse), and I dressed up as Santa Claus (my horse was Rudolph the Red Nosed Reindeer).

Claremont's horses stay in a barn called the Summer Barn during the two-day Junior Olympics show at Thomas School on Long Island. The barn has a roof but no walls. Our banner lets people know where Claremont's horses are stabled.

SUMMER BARN

You're up at the crack of dawn to compete in the Junior Olympics.

EARLY BIRD

The first time I rode in the Junior Olympics, I was really nervous. I didn't know what to expect. There was a lot of team spirit that year; everyone joined together in an effort to win for the barn. The second year I entered, I felt more relaxed . . . even though Quincy was pretty

frisky. Jenny, Audrey, and I, as a team, won the bronze medal for our division. We also won the first-prize cup for one of the jump classes.

On the first day of my second year at the Junior Olympics, I admired the trophy cups. I said to myself, "I really want to win one of those." And sure enough, Jenny, Audrey, and I did.

HOORAY!

At the Junior Olympics the three of us rode as a team the entire time. Our team had the fewest faults, or penalties. We came in first.

In the future, Chloe wants to raise horses or teach riding as a career.

ACKNOWLEDGMENTS

Many people have been of great help to *City Riders,* and I remain most grateful to the three stars of my book—Chloe, Audrey, and Jenny—and their parents, especially Chloe's dad;

Claremont Riding Academy, the setting for *City Riders,* and all the barn rats, trainers, and stable hands who agreed to be photographed;

Cindy Hahn of Leica Camera Group for providing additional Leica equipment for the project;

Katherine Pollack of Black & White for her assiduous work for the book; and Steven Gelber of Penguin Prints for coming through under a tight deadline.

Thank you to family and friends who have shown support for *City Riders,* particularly Doree Duncan Seligmann, computer whiz, who provided technical assistance at the outset of the project, and Aaron Barlow, whose computer became essential to the completion of the book.

I also salute horsewoman Julie Krone, whose presence and words remain an inspiration; and finally, I thank my editor, who encouraged my ideas.